This book is on loan from
Library Services for Schools

www.cumbria.gov.uk/libraries/schoolslibserv

County Council

The Human Body:

INVESTIGATING AN UNEXPLAINED DEATH

Andrew Solway

Raintree is an imprint of Capstone Global Library Limited, a company incorporated in England and Wales having its registered office at 7 Pilgrim Street, London, EC4V 6LB – Registered company number: 6695582

To contact Raintree, please phone 0845 6044371, fax + 44 (0) 1865 312263, or email myorders@ raintreepublishers.co.uk.

Text © Capstone Global Library Limited 2014
First published in hardback in 2014
The moral rights of the proprietor have been asserted.

Edited by Andrew Farrow, Adam Miller, and Adrian Vigliano
Designed by Richard Parker
Original illustrations © HL Studios
Illustrated by James Stayte (pages 4–7); HL Studios
Picture research by Ruth Blair
Production by Sophia Argyris
Originated by Capstone Global Library Ltd
Printed and bound in China by CTPS

ISBN 978 1 406 26105 9
17 16 15 14 13
10 9 8 7 6 5 4 3 2 1

British Library Cataloguing in Publication Data
Solway, Andrew
The human body: investigating an unexplained death.
– (Anatomy of an investigation)

A full catalogue record for this book is available from the British Library.

Acknowledgements

We would like to thank the following for permission to reproduce photographs: Alamy pp. 20 (© Science Photo Library), 28 (© Marmaduke St. John), 31 (© Science Photo Library), 43 (© Chris Rout); Capstone Publishers p. 48 (© Karon Dubke); Corbis pp. 16 (© Jim Sugar), 17 (© Photo Quest Ltd/Science Photo Library), 24 (© Peter MacDiarmid/Reuters), 38 (© moodboard); Courtesy of Glessner House Museum p. 35; Getty Images pp. 9 (Dan Kitwood), 12 (Christopher Furlong), 13 (Foto24/Gallo Images), 21 (xbn83), 37 (Peter Dazeley), 49 (Steve Gschmeissner/ SPL), 45 (Vince Bucci/AFP), 46 (Ron P. Jaffe/CBS Photo Archive), 47 (Echo); Science Photo Library p. 39 (R.E. Litchfield); Shutterstock pp. 20 (© DTKUTOO), 20 (© vetpathologist), 25 (© javi_indy), 36 (© Pete Niesen), 44 (© william casey), 11 (© HeinSchlebusch), 11 (© HeinSchlebusch), 41 (© Robert Kneschke), 41 (© Firma V), 11 (© Robert Kneschke); Superstock pp. 14 (BlueMoon Stock), 15 (David Scharf), 26 (Kallista Images), 30 (Corbis), 32 (Science and Society).

Cover photograph reproduced with permission of Corbis (© Ocean).

We would like to thank David Wright for his invaluable help in the preparation of this book.

Every effort has been made to contact copyright holders of any material reproduced in this book. Any omissions will be rectified in subsequent printings if notice is given to the publisher.

Contents

Some words are printed in bold, **like this**. You can find out what they mean by looking in the glossary on page 52.

DEATH IN CLARENCE CRESCENT

Police officers Khan and Fletcher are on night patrol. So far, it has been very quiet...

Hey, Jamal, that's just up the road!

...we have a report of gunshots at the following address: 52 Clarence Crescent...

We heard gunshots! About an hour ago. It sounded like they came from the flat downstairs. Mr and Mrs Boyd's place...

Open up, please, it's the police!

Looks like we'll have to force open the door.

Hello? Mr Boyd? Mrs Boyd? Oh, no...

Officer Khan is used to crime scenes, but this one is pretty bad. He walks in very carefully, trying to avoid the blood.

The SoCOs arrive.

EXTRACTS FROM THE MEDICAL EXAMINER'S REPORT

It looks as if there are two deaths.

* Is it a double suicide?
* Is it a murder?
* Is there any way it could have been an accident?

This is the story of how a team of police officers and scientists might find the answers in real life. Along the way, you will learn a lot about how the human body works.

Real-life CSI

If you have ever watched TV programmes or films about crimes, you will know that evidence from the crime scene is very important. This book looks at how crime scene investigations (**CSIs**) work in real life, and how human biology and science help to provide important evidence in crime investigations.

A scientific process

A crime investigation is similar to a scientific investigation. From an initial **assessment** of the scene, police may get an idea of what has happened. This is similar to a scientific **hypothesis**. They gather evidence from the crime scene and from other sources (for example, from interviews or research), and then they analyse this to see if it fits their hypothesis. If it does not fit, the hypothesis may be wrong.

For example, police may have an initial hypothesis that a person found dead in a house committed **suicide**. But then analysis of some blood found at the scene shows that it is **blood group** AB, while the victim had blood group O (for more on blood groups, see pages 26 and 27). The **evidence** suggests that another person was at the crime scene. The initial hypothesis needs to be changed.

CRIME SCENE MANAGER

The crime scene managers make sure that evidence from the crime scene is properly collected.

This is essential if the police investigation is to be a fair test. Their first job is to seal off the crime scene so that no one can interfere with or **contaminate** the evidence. This could mean sealing off a room, a house or flat, or a whole street.

Next, a crime scene manager does an initial assessment. This involves deciding which evidence to collect, and what order to collect it in. Some evidence is very time-sensitive. Footprints or tyre tracks on wet ground, for example, must be photographed before they are damaged or washed away.

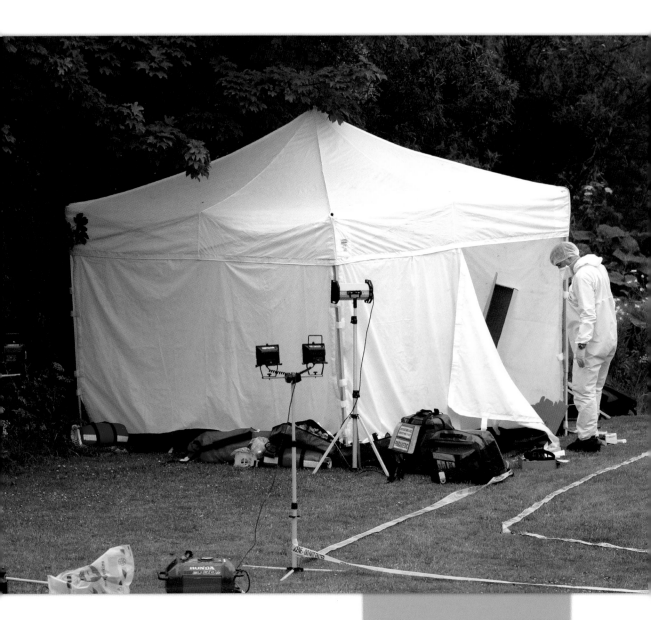

A crime scene outdoors is harder to protect than one in a house or other building. It is common for police to put up a tent to keep the area dry and to screen it from view.

Alive or dead?

Once they have called for back-up, Officer Khan assesses the crime scene. He needs to check that no one else is there. He keeps his hands in his pockets, to stop himself from picking things up. He avoids the main walking areas, to preserve footprints. Under the table in one corner, he finds a third body, covered in blood. After the **medical examiner** arrives, she checks and finds that the third victim is alive! The ambulance rushes him off for emergency treatment.

How do we know if someone is dead?

When people die, all their body functions stop. They stop breathing, so no oxygen gets into their blood. The heart stops beating, so the blood no longer carries food and oxygen to the cells. Once the body's cells are starved of food and oxygen, they soon stop working.

However, it is not always easy to tell if someone is dead. The medical examiner has to check carefully for signs of life. To check whether the heart and lungs are working, the medical examiner:

- listens to the heart for one minute
- feels for a **pulse** for one minute
- checks for signs of breathing.

If the heart and breathing stop for a short time, a person can survive. So, to be certain, the medical examiner also checks for brain activity. She carries out the following tests:

- She looks at the pupils (openings in the centre of the eye) to check if there is a response to a shining light. In a living person, the pupils get smaller in bright light.
- She rubs hard on the breastbone (sternum). This is very painful, and if the **nervous system** is working, a person will react to the pain.

Death and the brain stem

A person is considered to be dead if the brain stem - the part of the brain that controls automatic processes such as breathing and digestion - is no longer active.

YOU'RE THE INVESTIGATOR!

Look at this report from the medical examiner. Based on this report, how can we tell which of the victims are dead and which are alive? (Find the answer on page 12.)

Medical examiner's report

NAME: Boyd, Anne
Initial examination: White female, 36 years old. Signs of multiple gunshot wounds to head and chest. Evidence of extensive blood loss. No discernible heartbeat or pulse after one minute. No signs of breathing. No response to light shone in pupil or rubbing of sternum.

NAME: Boyd, James
Initial examination: White male, 39 years old. Gunshot wounds to head and abdomen. Evidence of some blood loss. No discernible heartbeat or pulse after one minute. No signs of breathing. No response to light shone in pupil or rubbing of sternum.

NAME: unknown
Initial examination: Hispanic male, 24 years old. Evidence of head trauma and extensive blood loss. Faint heartbeat and very shallow, irregular breathing.

Collecting, documenting, and protecting the scene

Once the ambulance has taken away the injured man, the **Scene of Crime Officers (SoCOs)** get to work. Their job is to document the crime scene and to collect any evidence that might help with the investigation.

Documenting a crime scene means writing descriptions of how the scene looks, making sketches, and taking photographs. The photographer starts by taking long-range photos of the whole scene, then focuses in to take close-ups of things such as the positions of bodies, weapons, bloodstains, and any other details that might be important.

SoCOs wear gloves, boots, and full protective coveralls at a crime scene. Protective clothes stop the SoCOs from contaminating the crime scene. They also help to protect the investigators from being exposed to any dangerous materials at the crime scene.

SoCOs wear disposable coveralls with a hood, disposable overshoes, latex gloves, and a face mask. This prevents the investigators themselves from contaminating the site with fingerprints, fibres, or other traces.

Once the crime scene has been documented, the SoCOs start collecting evidence. This can be clothing, weapons, samples of blood, hairs, fibres, footprints, tyre tracks, tool marks, paint chips – anything that might be a clue. The final job is to dust for fingerprints. This is left until last, because the dusting powder makes a mess and contaminates the scene.

YOU'RE THE INVESTIGATOR!: THE ANSWER

Look back at the medical examiner's report on page 11. Mr and Mrs Boyd are both dead. They have no heartbeat or pulse, no signs of breathing, and they show no response to light or to rubbing the sternum. The third victim has a heartbeat and is breathing, so he is alive.

SoCO equipment

The following equipment is essential for SoCOs:

- *Protective gear:* Protective suits, overshoes, and gloves are needed to prevent the contamination of a crime scene while collecting evidence.
- *Camera:* A camera is essential equipment for documenting a scene.
- *Notebook and pens:* Notebooks and pens are used for taking notes and sketching the scene.
- *Sticky tape:* Sticky tape can be used for lifting some kinds of fingerprints and footprints.
- *Casting materials:* Casting materials are needed for making casts of footprints, tyre tracks, and so on.
- *Swabs:* Swabs are used for collecting blood samples.
- *Enhancement chemicals:* Enhancement chemicals are used to make blood, fingerprints, and other things show up in colour or in special lighting.
- *Collection bags, containers, and labels:* These are needed for storing evidence safely on its way back to the **forensics** lab.

These cases of equipment, microscope, and books are the type of items used by crime scene investigators.

Using the senses

Searching a crime scene involves sight, smell, and touch. Many pieces of evidence are found by looking for them. However, SoCOs often do fingertip searches for very small objects, because we can sometimes feel objects that we cannot see.

The smell at a crime scene can be very strong. When people die, their bodies begin to **decompose** (rot), which produces unpleasant smells. Sometimes a dead body is only discovered when people notice the smell.

The police investigate

The police's investigative team is made up of the detectives who have to work out what happened. Did Mr and Mrs Boyd kill themselves? It seems unlikely, now that there is a third person involved. So, what did happen?

The SoCOs have collected a lot of evidence, but it is not of much use yet. The evidence has to go to the forensics lab to be analysed. Meanwhile, police detectives start following up on other leads. Who were Mr and Mrs Boyd? What did they do? Who were their friends and relatives? Some officers search the flat, while others start knocking on the neighbours' doors.

POLICE DETECTIVES

The detectives on the police team are in charge of the overall investigation of the crime.

Police detectives gather information from a wide variety of sources. These include the crime scene itself, anyone at the crime scene, people in the surrounding area, the family and friends of the victims, and information from police databases or from other police operations. The investigators look at all the evidence and try to draw conclusions.

Police detectives often get useful information by interviewing people living near the crime scene or people who regularly pass through the area.

Forensic science

SoCOs only collect evidence. They do not do any analysis of what they find. That is the job of the forensics lab.

Forensic science (forensics) is the use of science in any kind of situation involving the law. For example, a forensic scientist might check the **DNA** of one or more men to help identify the father of a child.

The basis of forensics at a crime scene is that humans leave traces wherever they go. Anyone coming into a crime scene might leave behind bits of dead skin, pollen, fibres from clothes, fingerprints, footprints, or **saliva** (spit) on a cup or a glass. When they leave the scene, they take new traces with them – for example, fibres from the carpet. Forensic science can help to identify these traces.

Learning from the dead

The bodies of Mr and Mrs Boyd are sent for **autopsies**. The **pathologist** looks for evidence of how they died. Mrs Boyd has six bullet wounds: four to the body and two to the head. One of the bullets is still in her head. Mr Boyd has eight bullet wounds. Two bullets are embedded (stuck) in his spine. The pathologist sends all the bullets for analysis.

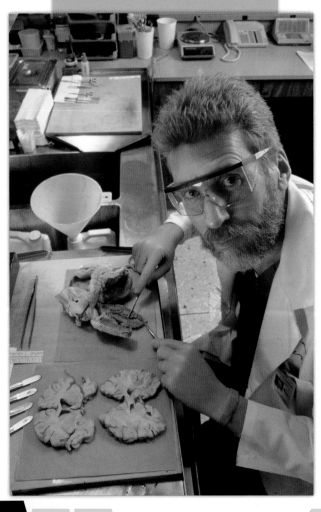

As part of the postmortem. pathologists take out the body organs and cut them into sections to examine them. This pathologist is examining the brain.

A PROTECTIVE LAYER

The skin is only a very thin covering on the body, but it manages to do several different jobs:

- The skin is thick enough to be a physical barrier against tiny living things called micro-organisms.

- **Glands** in the skin produce oils, which help to make it waterproof. The waterproofing is mainly to keep water in, rather than to keep it out. Without it, we would have to live in damp places or drink far more often.

- There is a network of capillaries (small blood vessels) in the lower layers of the skin. When it is warm, blood is diverted to these capillaries to help the body lose heat. When it is cold, the capillaries can be shut down to help keep the heat in.

- **Pigments** in the skin help to protect the body from ultraviolet (UV) radiation from the Sun, which can damage body **tissues**.

The epidermis

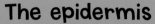

The epidermis is the top layer of the skin. The outer layers of the epidermis are made up of dead cells. Throughout our lives, we are constantly shedding dead cells from the outer epidermis. We lose around a million skin cells every day.

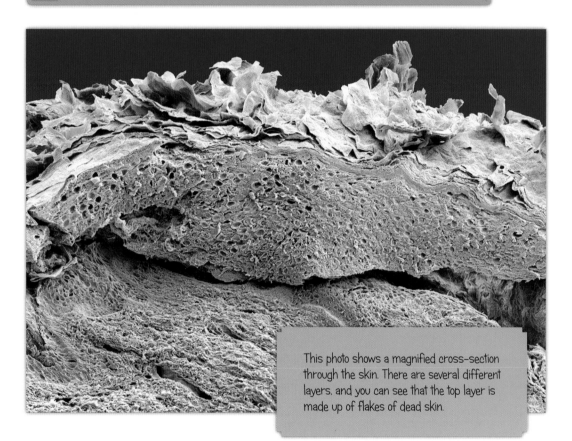

This photo shows a magnified cross-section through the skin. There are several different layers, and you can see that the top layer is made up of flakes of dead skin.

Performing an autopsy

If a death is suspicious or the cause is not clear, the body is sent for an autopsy. A surgeon called a forensic pathologist performs the autopsy. So, what does an autopsy involve?

The first job is to examine the outside of the body. Bruising, a rash, or other marks on the skin can indicate injury, disease, or poisoning. There may also be larger wounds caused by bullets, a knife, or some other weapon.

Body organs

In the second stage of the autopsy, pathologists cut through the skin and examine the organs inside the body. They then remove the heart, brain, and other organs. They look for damage caused by a wound or for signs of poisons or drugs. Are any of the organs damaged enough to cause death?

In the case of the Boyds, the pathologist finds that Mrs Boyd's brain was seriously damaged by bullet wounds. Mr Boyd's heart, brain, and spine were all badly damaged by bullets.

Organ systems

Our bodies rely on a number of specialized organs. Each of these organs has a particular job to do. For example, the heart is an organ that pumps blood around the body. The brain is the body's main control centre. The lungs are where the blood system can take up oxygen from the air.

The organs are organized so that they work together in systems.

The heart is part of the **circulatory system**, along with the blood vessels. The blood vessels carry oxygen and nutrients to the body cells, and they carry away carbon dioxide and wastes, which will be excreted (released as waste).

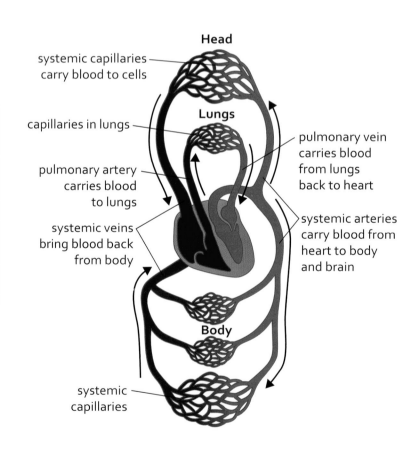

Head

systemic capillaries carry blood to cells

capillaries in lungs

Lungs

pulmonary vein carries blood from lungs back to heart

pulmonary artery carries blood to lungs

systemic veins bring blood back from body

systemic arteries carry blood from heart to body and brain

Body

systemic capillaries

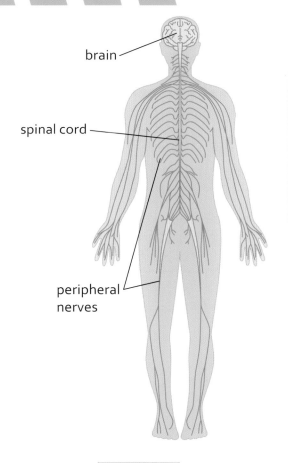

brain

spinal cord

peripheral nerves

The brain is part of the nervous system, along with the spinal cord and **nerves**. Nerves carry information about our surroundings to the brain, which processes the information. It then sends out signals along other nerves to organs such as muscles, making the body react to what is happening around it. The brain also controls processes inside the body such as breathing, digestion, and changes in heart rate.

Case study: bones and teeth

Information about bones and teeth collected during an autopsy can help to identify a person. In one case in California, police found seven bodies buried in a backyard. They thought that they knew who the victims were, but the individual bodies were hard to identify. The pathologist arranged to take X-rays of each victim's bones and matched them with X-rays taken when the people were alive. Of course, this relies upon having past records available!

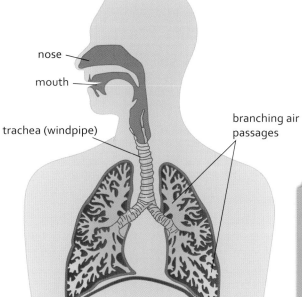

nose

mouth

trachea (windpipe)

branching air passages

The lungs are part of the **respiratory system**, along with the nose, mouth, and windpipe. This system draws in fresh air from the outside that is rich in oxygen. The body cells need the oxygen in order to get energy. The respiratory system also gets rid of carbon dioxide, which is a waste gas produced in the cells.

Under the microscope

The pathologist is fairly sure how Mr and Mrs Boyd died. However, he does some additional checks to be certain. He takes small pieces of tissue and looks at them under the microscope. Are there other signs or damage or disease that could have led to death – or example, from a heart attack?

Tissues and cells

Organs are made up of several different tissues. The heart, for example, has a large amount of muscle tissue, some lining (epithelial) tissue, and some connective tissue, while the brain is made mainly of nervous (nerve) tissue.

Each tissue is made up of much smaller units: cells. Cells are the building blocks of living things, and there are several different types of them. Each tissue is made of cells of the same type. All of the cells in a tissue work together to do a particular job, or function.

The cells in different tissues are specialized for their functions. Muscle cells are long, thin cells that can contract (shorten). Nerve cells have extensions (nerve fibres) that can carry electrical signals. Red blood cells are full of the pigment hemoglobin, which can combine with and carry oxygen.

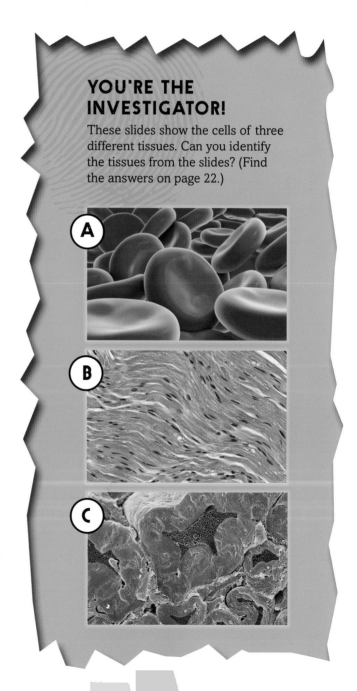

YOU'RE THE INVESTIGATOR!

These slides show the cells of three different tissues. Can you identify the tissues from the slides? (Find the answers on page 22.)

A

B

C

Telling the time

As soon as people die, their bodies begin to change. Based on these changes, the pathologist can estimate when a person died.

One early change is rigor mortis, which is when the muscles of the body stiffen and become rigid due to a chemical imbalance (lack of something called ATP) in the muscle cells. The onset of this varies from person to person, but it generally lasts from about an hour or two after death until around 24 hours after death, and then it starts to disappear.

Over a longer period, the body begins to decompose. Tiny living things called bacteria and fungi from the intestines begin to spread and break down body tissues. At the same time, **enzymes** and other chemicals within cells begin to break them down from the inside.

If a body is not found quickly, animals will begin to eat the body tissues. Blowflies are insects that lay their eggs in dead tissue. The larvae (maggots) hatch after one to two days and begin to feed on the flesh. In the outdoors, rodents, foxes, dogs, and birds such as vultures will also feed on a dead body.

Flesh flies are another type of fly that feeds on rotting flesh. They can be recognized by their red eyes and the grey stripes along their bodies.

Autopsy report

The pathologist has finished the autopsies. He has found that Mr and Mrs Boyd were killed by gunshot wounds. He thinks that the Boyds were dead for at least six hours before they were found. But the neighbours reported hearing gunshots only an hour before the police arrived. This will need to be investigated further.

Drug tests

If pathologists think that a death may have been caused or contributed to by poison or drugs, they may send off blood and tissue samples for testing.

YOU'RE THE INVESTIGATOR!: THE ANSWER

Look back at the question on page 20. Here are the answers:

a) red blood cells   b) muscle tissue   c) brain tissue

Some drugs are given by doctors to treat illness. Some other drugs, such as alcohol, can be used legally by adults. Other drugs, such as marijuana and cocaine, are illegal.

All kinds of drugs can have effects that could lead to illness and death. For example, many people die on the roads each year because they drive after they have been drinking alcohol. Medical drugs can also have effects that make it unsafe to drive. Some asthma drugs, for example, make people sleepy.

Alcohol is a depressant drug. Depressants do not necessarily make people feel depressed. In small doses, they can sometimes make people more relaxed. Larger doses can occasionally lead to sickness and unconsciousness. Sleeping pills are depressants, as are illegal drugs such as opium and morphine.

Stimulants are drugs that speed up the nervous system. Tea and coffee contain small amounts of the stimulant caffeine. Illegal drugs such as amphetamines, cocaine, and ecstasy are strong stimulants. They are known to make people take dangerous risks.

Hallucinogens are drugs that affect a person's senses. Illegal drugs such as LSD and ketamine are hallucinogens. Some people taking this kind of drug may feel extremely good for a time, but then they may become very tense and have panic attacks, cramps, and nausea. Most drugs also have longer-term health effects, such as depression, heart and lung problems, or liver disease.

YOU'RE THE INVESTIGATOR!

Below is the **toxicology** report for Mrs Boyd. The pathologist gets it back about a week after sending off the blood samples for analysis. Rohypnol is a fast-acting **sedative**. Its effects are even greater when it is mixed with alcohol.

- What kind of drug is a sedative?
- Two glasses were found on the table at the crime scene. What sort of test should be done on the glasses?

You can find the answer at the bottom of this page.

Toxicology involves testing the blood of a suspect or a victim for the presence of a range of drugs. This report shows the results for Mrs Boyd, including a positive (POS) test for a drug called Rohypnol.

ACUTE TOXICOLOGY TEST REPORT

Office of Chief Medical Officer
Felix House, Springfield Road

Margaret Hall, MD
Chief Medical Officer
Noel Barnes, PhD
Chief Toxicologist

Priority no. 3
Tox. no. 2706175-00

Name: BOYD, Anne
Case number: 9300546

Blood	Ethanol	NEG
Blood	Cannabinoids	NEG
Blood	Cocaine	NEG
Blood	Opiates	NEG
Blood	Benzodiazepines	POS
Blood	Amphetamines	NEG

Further tests: different benzodiazepines

Chlordiazepoxide (Librium)	NEG
Flunitrazepam (Rohypnol)	POS
Diazepam (Valium)	NEG
Alprazolam (Xanax)	NEG

Date: 12/6/10   Time: 3.40 p.m.
Released by: Beryl Anderson

Approval date: 14/6/10   Signature: *Noel Barnes*

YOU'RE THE INVESTIGATOR!: THE ANSWER

A sedative is a drug taken for its calming or sleep-inducing effects. The glasses on the table should be tested for fingerprints. There will also be traces of saliva on the glasses, which can be sent for DNA analysis.

Doing the forensics

The autopsy report gives the police their first real evidence from the crime scene. But there are no results yet from the forensics lab. Over 100 pieces of evidence were sent to the lab, plus hundreds of photos.

Fingerprint evidence

At a forensics lab, scientists and technicians analyse the evidence they receive from crime scenes. Some of the members of the team are specialists who might just look at fingerprints, DNA, or firearms.

The skin on our fingertips has a pattern of fine ridges that help us to grip things. The ridges are different for each person. These are our fingerprints.

Sometimes fingerprints are visible at a crime scene – for instance, they show as marks in blood. However, most fingerprints are latent, meaning they cannot be seen. We leave fingerprints everywhere, because our skin produces oils to help make it waterproof (see page 16). When CSI teams look for fingerprints, they dust hard surfaces with a very fine powder. The powder sticks to the oil and makes the fingerprints show up. Fingerprints from absorbent surfaces such as paper or cloth can be made visible using a chemical spray or lab treatments.

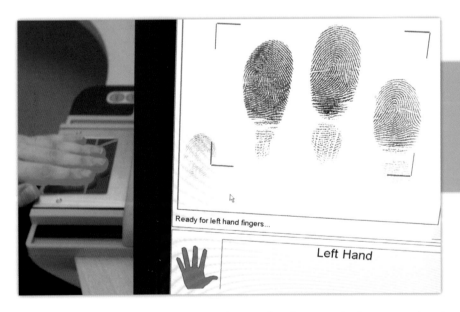

Ready for left hand fingers...

Left Hand

Fingerprints can now be taken using a scanner instead of the traditional inkpad and paper.

Once fingerprints are visible, they can be photographed or scanned and compared with known fingerprints. These might include the fingerprints of the victims, their friends and relatives, and fingerprints from a national database of known criminals.

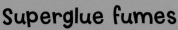

Superglue fumes

One way to make a permanent record of a fingerprint is with superglue. The object is placed in a closed chamber, and superglue vapour is passed over it for several hours. The superglue sticks to any fingerprints and forms a pattern of white ridges.

Glands and secretions

Oil on the skin is produced by glands. These are organs that produce secretions, which are liquids that are released outside cells. The body produces many different secretions. Sweat and tears are two other secretions from the skin. Inside the body, the nose, mouth, intestines, and airways produce mucus, which protects surfaces and acts as a lubricant (something that makes it easier for things to move). Glands in the intestines also produce digestive juices, which speed up the breakdown of food.

When we get hot, sweat glands in the skin produce a clear, slightly salty fluid called perspiration, or sweat. As the sweat evaporates, it helps to cool the body. People also sweat when they are nervous, excited, or afraid. In these situations, sweating is restricted to the palms, soles, armpits, and forehead.

Blood groups and spatter

There was a lot of blood at the crime scene, so there are many blood samples and photographs. A **hematologist** does the blood analysis, while another expert looks at the blood patterns.

Looking at blood

Blood is the main transportation system in the body. Red blood cells carry oxygen, which the cells need in order to produce energy. Cells also need food, mainly in the form of the sugar **glucose**. This is carried in the liquid part of the blood (the plasma).

Blood also has an important role in the body's immune system, which is the organ system that protects the body from disease and illness. White blood cells help to protect the body against infection and disease. The cells in the blood are covered with special markers called **antigens**. These markers help white blood cells to tell the difference between our own cells and an invader. Doctors can also use these antigens to recognize different types of blood, known as blood groups.

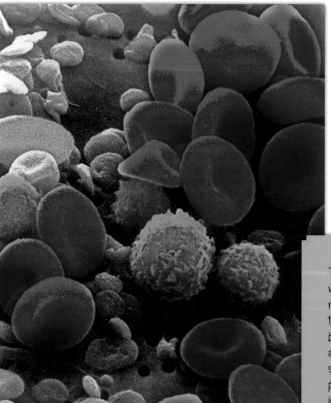

The most common system for classifying blood groups is called the ABO system. People with type A blood have A antigens on their blood cells. Those with type B blood have B antigens. Type AB blood has both A and B antigens, while type O has no antigens. Testing blood for ABO and other antigens can help identify which person a blood sample has come from.

This is a photo of blood taken with a scanning electron microscope. The red cells with the dip in the centre are red blood cells. The purple cells are white blood cells. The small yellow shapes are platelets, which are involved in blood clotting.

Spatter patterns

An expert can tell a lot about what happened at a crime scene from the blood patterns found there. Blood that sprays out at high speed leaves a different pattern from blood that simply drops onto a surface. This can show whether the blood came from a knife or from a bullet wound.

It is also possible to work out the angle at which blood hits a surface. The more elongated the drop is, the shallower the angle of impact.

YOU'RE THE INVESTIGATOR!

The diagram here shows three blood drops from the crime scene. The angle at which a drop hits is related to the width of the drop (the smaller measurement), divided by its length.

The table gives the angle of impact for different width to length ratios. Work out the angles for the three blood drops. (You can find the answer on page 28.)

Ratio of width to length (width divided by length)	Angle of blood drop to surface
0.09	5°
0.17	10°
0.26	15°
0.34	20°
0.42	25°
0.50	30°
0.64	40°
0.87	60°
0.94	70°
1.00	90°

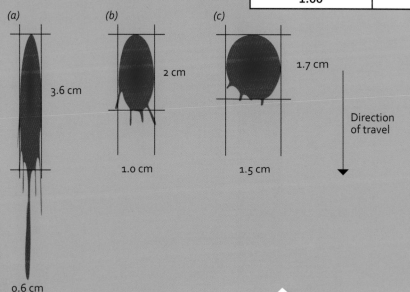

(a) 3.6 cm / 0.6 cm

(b) 2 cm / 1.0 cm

(c) 1.7 cm / 1.5 cm

Direction of travel

Analysing the ballistics

The blood analysis has found blood from four people at the crime scene: the blood of the three victims, plus an unknown fourth sample. The unknown sample has been sent to another lab for DNA analysis.

Now the **ballistics** evidence is coming through...

This photo shows a ballistics expert test-firing a gun into a water tank. The water is more resistant than air, and slows down the bullet before it reaches the end of the tank. The resulting bullet has a "fingerprint" of markings from the barrel of the gun it was fired from. These markings can be compared with those on any bullets found at the crime scene.

BALLISTICS EXPERT

Ballistics experts usually have a background in physics. They use some of the physics you learn in school to work out the trajectories (flight paths) of bullets.

How do they make their assessments? Until it hits something, the main forces on a speeding bullet are the downward pull of gravity and a backward force (drag) from air resistance. The speed of the bullet and its mass (weight) affect how far the bullet can penetrate through a body or other barrier.

Ballistics

Ballistics is the science of how bullets and other projectiles (objects projected by a force) fly through the air. Working out the flight paths of bullets can supply useful information about where a gun was fired. Forensic firearms experts also use small marks on bullets and inside gun barrels to match up bullets with the guns that fired them. If a gun is thought to have been used in a shooting, firearms experts do test shootings to check if any bullets found at the crime scene were fired by that gun.

When a gun is fired, it gives off a small cloud of powder and gases. Some of this gunshot **residue** lands on the person firing the gun. Forensics teams can test suspects for gunshot residue on the clothes and the skin.

This is the ballistics report on the gun and three of the bullets found at the crime scene.

FORENSICS LABORATORY

323 Investigations Way
Manchester

BALLISTICS REPORT

Case no: 9300546
Priority no. 3

Gun EX1 found at scene. Semi-automatic pistol, 0.452 in., M1911 copy of unknown manufacture.

Bullet Q1, found in skull of female. 0.357 in. diameter, FMJ. **Calibre** of ammunition not compatible with gun found at scene.

Bullets Q2 and Q3, found in spine of male. 0.452 in. diameter, FMJ. Comparisons of markings suggest that Q2 and Q3 were fired from the same gun.

YOU'RE THE INVESTIGATOR!

Look at this report from the ballistics team. Do the bullets match with the gun found in the flat? (You can find the answer on page 31.)

Evidence starts to come in

The ballistics evidence is very interesting. Two guns were used to kill the Boyds. The gun found at the crime scene killed Mr Boyd. Another gun, which fired different bullets, was used to kill Mrs Boyd. There was no gunshot residue on either Mr or Mrs Boyd. This strongly suggests that neither of them fired a gun.

More evidence has come back from forensics. The fingerprints at the crime scene included those of Mrs Boyd's father and mother and of four neighbours. Broken glass found in the kitchen was from a wine glass. There were traces of wine on some pieces and saliva on others. The wine and saliva are sent for analysis.

Wound recovery

Mr and Mrs Boyd were killed by their gunshot wounds. A gunshot causes serious damage all along the path of the bullet and can damage organs and tissues nearby. However, people can recover from gunshot wounds and other serious injuries.

Often people need surgery after a gunshot wound. The surgeon cleans up the injury site, stops bleeding, and closes up the wound as much as possible. But it is the body itself that actually repairs the wound.

The first stage of recovery is inflammation, which is when the wound area swells up. Much of the swelling is caused by fluid from the blood leaking into the area. In this fluid, there are white blood cells, which help to fight off any infection.

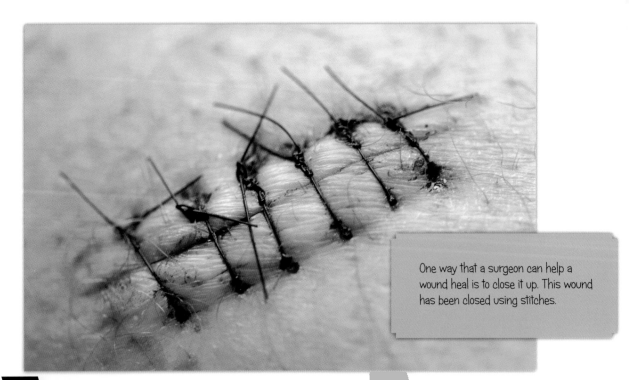

One way that a surgeon can help a wound heal is to close it up. This wound has been closed using stitches.

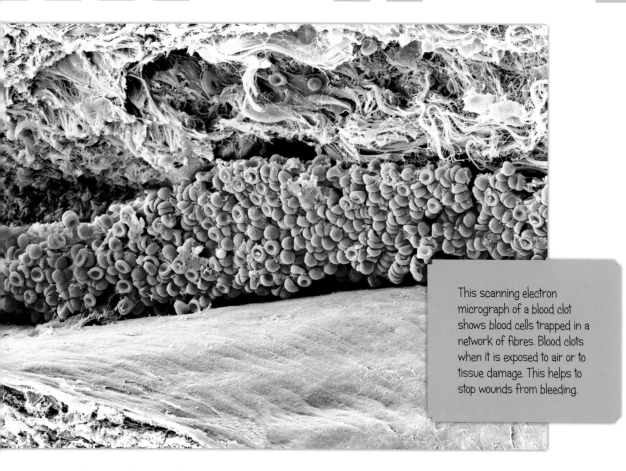

This scanning electron micrograph of a blood clot shows blood cells trapped in a network of fibres. Blood clots when it is exposed to air or to tissue damage. This helps to stop wounds from bleeding.

In the second stage of recovery, a blood clot forms, sealing the wound. Blood vessels start to mend themselves and new scar tissue starts to form. The scar tissue provides temporary protection for the wound area.

The final stage of recovery involves rebuilding damaged tissue. This can take years. Often the body cannot repair itself completely, leaving the person with some permanent damage and some scar tissue.

YOU'RE THE INVESTIGATOR!: THE ANSWER

Look back at the box and ballistic report on page 29. The report shows that the bullets that killed Mr Boyd came from the gun found at the crime scene. However, the bullet found in Mrs Boyd was a different calibre (size). The gun found at the scene could not have fired this bullet.

DNA testing

The unknown blood sample from the Boyds' flat has been sent for DNA profiling. Blood tests can only give a partial indication of whether blood is from a particular person. However, analysing the DNA in a blood sample gives a unique "fingerprint", or DNA profile. The saliva sample from the broken wine glass is also tested for DNA.

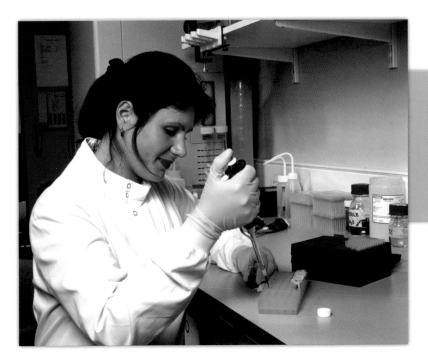

DNA tests can be done on very small samples of material. A technique called the polymerase chain reaction (PCR) makes it possible to copy the DNA many times before it is analysed.

DNA fingerprinting

Over 99 per cent of our DNA is the same as everyone else's. However, there are short sections of DNA that vary from person to person. **DNA fingerprinting** works by comparing several of these short sections.

Passing on instructions

DNA – the **genetic material** – is what makes it possible for living things to reproduce. It is found in the nucleus of every living cell. In humans, the genetic material is 23 pairs of **chromosomes** – 46 in all. A chromosome is one incredibly long molecule of DNA.

The genetic material contains all the "instructions" needed for a living thing to grow from a single cell. During sexual reproduction, each parent passes on one "set" of genetic instructions (23 chromosomes) to the new child.

DNA structure

Each DNA molecule is a double chain of millions of small sub-units known as bases. There are only four different bases, but these can be repeated many times. It is the specific order of the bases along a DNA molecule that holds information. The four bases are like letters in an alphabet. They form a long sequence of three-letter "words" along the length of the DNA. The order of the bases (and so the "words") is different along each chromosome.

Some sections of DNA form specific instructions called genes. The human body has tens of thousands of these genetic instructions.

	Suspect 1
	Suspect 2
	Swab 1
	Victim's blood
	Swab 2
	Suspect 3

This diagram shows DNA profiles from six blood samples in a crime investigation.

YOU'RE THE INVESTIGATOR!

The photo shows DNA fingerprinting profiles from six blood samples from a crime investigation. They are:
(a) blood from Suspect 1
(b) blood from Suspect 2
(c) a swab of blood from the crime scene (Swab 1)
(e) the victim's blood
(f) another swab of blood from the crime scene (Swab 2)
(g) blood from Suspect 3
Do any of the DNA profiles match up? (You can find the answer on page 35.)

Developments in the case

DNA analysis shows that the saliva on the wine glass is unknown. It does not match any DNA in the police database. However, the DNA does match with the DNA from the unknown blood sample.

The investigating officers ask Mrs Boyd's relatives, friends, and everyone in the block of flats for a saliva sample. The forensics lab does DNA profiles of each saliva sample and compares them with the mystery DNA.

The sleeper has awoken

While the saliva is being tested, the investigators get a piece of news. The third victim, who was unconscious, has woken up and is well enough to be interviewed. Two detectives visit the hospital to talk to him.

The man is named Esteban, and he was a friend of Mr and Mrs Boyd. He visited them on the evening of the murder and found their door open. He went in, closed the door, and found the couple dead. Esteban went over to the telephone to call the police. However, he slipped in some blood and fell, hitting his head on the corner of the table and knocking himself out.

There is evidence to support Esteban's story. A blood smear on the carpet could have been made by someone slipping. The corner of the table has Esteban's blood on it. And Esteban had only one wound, on the head, which could have been caused by the table corner. However, the police still keep Esteban on their suspect list.

Interpreting evidence

Like scientists, the police have to be careful how they interpret evidence. In this case, for example, there is evidence to suggest that Esteban did slip on some blood, fall, and hit his head. However, the evidence does not show *when* this happened. It is possible that Esteban killed the Boyds and then slipped by accident.

THE NUTSHELL STUDIES

In the 1940s, a wealthy American doctor called Frances Glessner Lee made a series of detailed, doll-sized crime scenes to use for training medical examiners and police officers in Chicago, USA. The Nutshell Studies, as they were called, were designed to improve the trainees' powers of observation and their ability to interpret evidence.

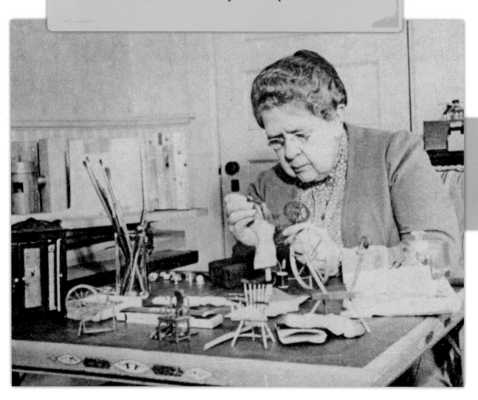

Frances Glessner Lee making a figure for one of her Nutshell murder studies.

YOU'RE THE INVESTIGATOR!: THE ANSWER

Look back at the box and the DNA profiles on page 33. The DNA profiles of Swab 1 and Suspect 3 are very similar. It would need to be checked, but it seems very likely that one blood sample found at the crime scene was from Suspect 3.

The importance of police work

The police investigators have gathered all kinds of information from people in the flats. The couple who reported the crime, Mr Smith and Ms Lin, said they heard gunshots late at night. Other neighbours said they heard loud noises earlier in the evening.

All the people in the flats are happy to give saliva samples for DNA testing – except one. At one flat, a man answers the door and seems uneasy. When officers ask for a saliva sample, the man makes a run for it. Several officers chase him, but he gets away.

Adrenaline is not just released in an emergency. We produce adrenaline any time the body goes into action.

Chemical messengers

When the human body suddenly has to go into action, many organ systems start working at once. The nervous system sends out signals telling the muscles to get working. Soon the circulatory system and the respiratory system are also busy, keeping the muscles supplied with oxygen and glucose. Another system becomes involved, too. This is the endocrine system, which produces **hormones**.

Hormones are chemical messengers. They are produced by glands and released into the blood, which allows them to circulate around the body. Some organs or tissues, called the target organs or tissues, take up the hormone. It then has an effect on the way those organs or tissues work.

Fight or flight

Suppose you are walking home one evening and you see a gang of people with knives coming towards you. Without thinking, you start to run as fast as you can away from the gang.

In an emergency like this, the body releases a hormone called **adrenaline**. Adrenaline is the "fight or flight" hormone, because it gets the body ready to go into action. Adrenaline increases the heart rate and the force of the heartbeat. It acts to expand the blood vessels so that the blood can flow more quickly. It also acts on the liver, which breaks down stored carbohydrates (the main energy food source) into glucose. The glucose is released into the blood, to make sure the body has plenty of energy.

People with severe allergies can die of shock if they have an allergic reaction, which is when the immune system reacts to a substance to cause effects such as sneezing or low blood pressure. To help them survive, some allergy sufferers carry something called an EpiPen. This is a syringe that they can use to inject a controlled dose of adrenaline into the blood. The extra boost they get from the adrenaline can save their life.

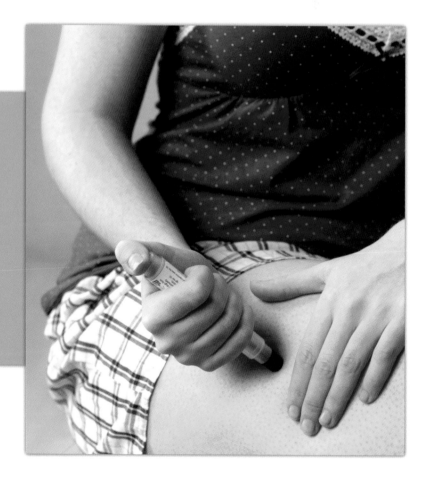

Closing in

The police pick up the runaway man a few days later. He does not want to give a DNA sample, and the police cannot force him. However, an officer offers the man a cigarette, and he takes it. Later, the police get enough saliva from the cigarette stub to run a DNA test.

A dead end

When the police get the DNA results from the cigarette stub, they find that the DNA does not match with the unknown blood sample or the saliva found at the crime scene. However, there is a match in the police DNA database. The man's name is Dave Stratton, and he is wanted for several robberies, which is why he fled. But he is not connected with the murders.

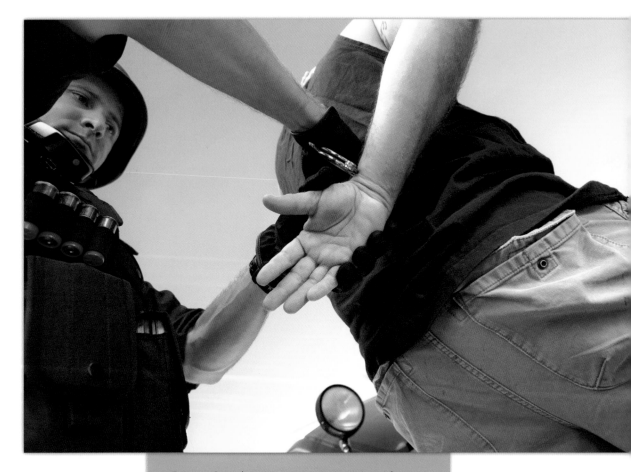

Evidence from the crime scene investigation and from forensic tests has been crucial in helping the police to make an arrest.

Fibre forensics

Now **trace evidence** is coming in from forensics. A partial footprint in some blood had carpet fibres sticking to it. The fibres are not from carpets in the Boyds' flat. They seem to match with carpets found in all the upstairs flats.

This latest piece of evidence fits in with a theory that the police investigators have been working on. The police think that Mr Smith and Ms Lin murdered the Boyds. The couple went to the Boyds' flat for a drink and put Rohypnol in Mr and Mrs Boyd's wine. Once both of them were sleepy from the drug, Mr Smith and Ms Lin shot the Boyds. They washed the wine glasses, but somehow one got left out of the dishwasher. They left a gun next to Mrs Boyd's body, to make it look like suicide.

The police investigators are waiting for the DNA evidence from the saliva samples to confirm their suspicions. If the saliva from either Mr Smith or Ms Lin is a match for the unknown blood sample, the police will have a strong case.

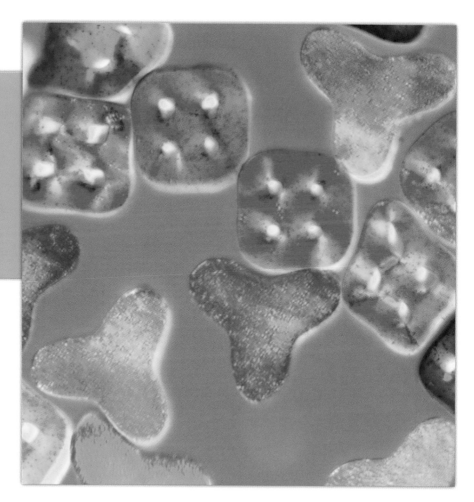

A polarized light micrograph of two different types of carpet fibre. One set of fibres are square in cross-section and have hollow space in them. The other fibres are solid and have a trilobal (three-lobed) shape.

Making a case

One piece of evidence is not enough to prove that a person or people carried out a crime. There may be several other pieces of evidence that point to a different person or people. Investigators must make a convincing case that takes into account all the evidence. If the **public prosecutor**'s office thinks that the case is strong enough, the case will go to court.

YOU'RE THE INVESTIGATOR!

This evidence board shows the information that the police have gathered so far. They think they have almost enough evidence to make a case. What do *you* think happened, judging from the evidence? You can find the answer on page 42.

On most crime investigations, the police investigation team use an evidence board as a way to display and organize information and ideas. The police's evidence board for the Boyd murder case could have looked something like this.

Suspects
- Esteban?
- Neighbours?
- Relatives?
- Dave Stratton?

Victims

Pathology

Mr and Mrs Boyd: killed by gunshot wounds
Time of death estimated around 7 p.m.
Blood of both victims tested positive for Rohypnol

Blood

Mr Boyd: AB. Mrs Boyd: O.
Esteban: O. Unknown: A.

Spatter patterns

Blood from Mr and Mrs Boyd: spatter from
high-speed projectile; some pooling
Blood from Esteban: spatter from sudden blow,
otherwise mostly pooling
Unknown: small spot on floor; vertical drip

Ballistics

Bullets of 2 calibres, .452 in. and .357 in.
Gun found at site .452 calibre. Fired shots
that killed Mr Boyd.
No gunshot residues on Boyds or Esteban.
Gun that killed Mrs Boyd not yet found.

Trace evidence

Fibres from footprint come from upstairs
flat.
Broken glass: wine glass pieces; same
manufacture as three other glasses
found in dishwasher

Evidence from police investigation

Interviews
• Boyds very popular
• Leading fight against demolition
of flats
• Differences in times when
shots heard

Research
• Jobs: Mr Boyd estate agent;
Mrs Boyd teacher; Ms Lin
property development;
Mr Smith insurance;
Esteban unemployed

DNA

4 blood samples: Mrs Boyd, Mr Boyd,
Esteban, fourth sample unknown
Saliva sample from wine glass:
same DNA as unknown blood
sample

YOU'RE THE INVESTIGATOR!: THE ANSWER

Have you decided what happened and who did it? Read on to find out
what the investigators have concluded.

Case closed

The evidence that the investigators have been waiting for has arrived. One of
the saliva samples from friends and neighbours has the same DNA profile as the
unknown blood sample and the saliva from the wine glass. It gives them enough
evidence to be fairly sure that their theory about how the Boyds died is correct.

Fitting the evidence

At first, the investigators thought the deaths were suicides. But then they found
new pieces of evidence:

- *A third person at the crime scene*: A third person (Esteban) was
  suspected of the crime, but he was later ruled out.

- *Blood from a fourth person*: This showed that at least one other person
  was at the crime scene besides the two people who were killed and the
  one who was injured.

- *The ballistics evidence*: Two different guns killed the Boyds. The Boyds did
  not fire either gun. The lack of gunshot residue on the third victim, Esteban,
  is strong evidence that he did not kill the Boyds.

- *The time of death*: The upstairs neighbours reported hearing gunshots late
  at night. The pathologist's report suggested that the Boyds died hours earlier.

- *Eyewitness accounts from other neighbours*: Other neighbours suggested
  that they heard loud noises earlier in the evening. This fits in better with the
  pathologist's report. It also undermines the testimony of Mr Smith and Ms.
  Lin, the neighbours who originally reported the crime.

- *The drug in the Boyds' blood*: Criminals often use Rohypnol, the drug found
  in the Boyds' blood, to sedate their victims.

- *The broken wine glass, plus the three other glasses in the dishwasher*:
  These suggest that four people drank wine together. The murderers could
  have used the wine to dose the Boyds with Rohypnol.

- *DNA evidence*: Blood and saliva found at the scene both have the same
  DNA profile. It indicates that a third person was in the kitchen and at the
  crime scene. The results from the saliva samples from relatives and
  neighbours showed that the DNA belonged to Mr Smith, the upstairs
  neighbour.

If Rohypnol is added to an alcoholic drink, it causes drowsiness, confusion, weakness, and memory loss. Putting Rohypnol in the Boyds' drinks would have made them less able to defend themselves if attacked.

Brought to justice

Once there is clear evidence against Mr Smith, police are able to search the upstairs flat. They find tiny traces of blood and gunshot residue on the shoes and clothes of Mr Smith and Ms Lin. However, there is no trace of the second gun.

The upstairs neighbours

With the evidence stacking up, the two neighbours admit they killed the Boyds. They did it because the Boyds were fighting plans to demolish the flats. The neighbours stood to make a lot of money if the flats were knocked down.

The final decision about who is guilty of a crime does not lie with the police. The police take their evidence to a criminal court. In court, the police's case is presented by a **barrister** for the prosecution. The arguments against the case are presented by the barrister for the defence. The barristers present evidence and question witnesses. A judge is in charge of the court. His or her job is to make sure that the case is fairly presented on each side.

The final decision about whether someone is innocent or guilty is made by a jury. This is a group of ordinary people brought in to decide on the outcome.

In this fictitious case, the two neighbours confessed they were guilty of the crime, so they would almost certainly be found guilty. Forensic evidence and evidence from the autopsies also form an important part of the police case.

An investigation collects evidence to determine the course of events. If that evidence is collected properly and convinces a jury, the person who committed the crime will be found guilty and punished.

The O.J. Simpson case

Occasionally, the police or forensic experts do get things wrong. It can mean that their evidence is not accepted in court. In 1994, Nicole Brown Simpson and her friend Ronald Goldman were murdered at Nicole's home. Nicole was the ex-wife of American football star O.J. Simpson.

Detectives found many pieces of evidence suggesting that O.J. Simpson carried out the murders. They found a glove, a hat, a sock, footprints, hair, and fibres linked to Simpson at the scene, as well as blood on his car and leading into his house. However, Simpson was found not guilty because the police made many errors in collecting, recording, and storing the evidence.

O.J. Simpson shows the jury a pair of gloves similar to the glove found at the scene where Nicole Brown Simpson and Ronald Goldman were murdered. The defence team claimed that the gloves did not fit so the glove found at the scene could not have been Simpson's.

The true value of CSI

Police investigators have many sophisticated tools to help find the truth about unexplained deaths. Experts can take fingerprints from all kinds of surfaces and use computers to help scan a huge database of fingerprints for matches. Techniques for analysing DNA are automated, and so samples can be tested more quickly than in the past. Machines such as gas chromatographs make it possible to make a detailed chemical analysis of really tiny samples of material.

The sets for TV shows about CSI work are full of high-tech equipment. However, a high-tech laboratory alone is not enough to solve a crime.

People as well as machines

Most of the time, the evidence from a forensics laboratory can be relied upon. Forensic scientists are careful and thorough in their work. They use similar methods to those used in scientific investigations, so their results are a fair test of the evidence.

The O.J. Simpson case (see page 45) shows that in a few cases, police officers and technicians do a bad job of collecting and recording evidence. If this happens, the evidence becomes useless because it cannot be trusted. It is not a fair test.

Not all forensics

Although forensic evidence is an important part of police work, it is not the only kind of evidence. Expert evidence alone is not enough to put a criminal behind bars. Police investigations also involve checking information, interviewing people, asking questions, and doing research to find the answers.

Medical examiners, forensic scientists, CSI teams, fingerprint specialists, haematologists, pathologists, and investigating officers all deal with the human victims at crime scenes. Some of these people are highly trained specialists who have studied human biology and medicine in university. However, all crime scene investigators, even the most highly trained, still need the basic scientific knowledge of the human body that they first learned in school.

You learn a lot of the basic knowledge that you need to be a forensic scientist or a pathologist in the science lessons you have in school.

Investigation: collecting trace evidence

Forensics provides useful evidence because we leave traces wherever we go. In this experiment, you will collect trace evidence from a very suspicious character – yourself!

What you will need

- a clean white sheet
- a soft brush, if available
- a hairbrush or comb
- clear adhesive tape
- tweezers
- a microscope, if available

What to do

Stand in the middle of the sheet. Start off by lifting your feet up one at a time. Have you left footprints?

Now jump up and down a few times on the spot.

Brush down your clothes with your hands or with a soft brush, if you have one. Use a comb or hairbrush on your hair.

Wait for a few seconds for the dust to settle, then step carefully off the sheet.

Collecting traces

Look at the sheet. Can you find any traces on it? Use the tape to pick up really small pieces of "evidence", and use a pair of tweezers for larger pieces. Try to collect at least 20 separate pieces of evidence.

Look carefully at the trace evidence you have collected. If you have a microscope, examine the pieces under the microscope. Can you classify the different pieces of debris? For instance, there could be flakes of skin, hairs, fibres, food crumbs, and dust.

This piece of sticky tape shows how much fluff and hair you might collect from your investigation. Look at your tape under a microscope to help identify the different pieces on it.

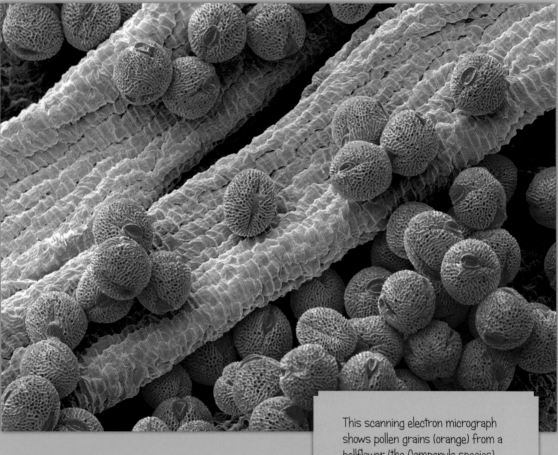

This scanning electron micrograph shows pollen grains (orange) from a bellflower (the Campanula species). You might find things like this in the traces you collect.

Presenting the results

Draw up a table you can use to write down your results. Think about what columns and rows you need in the table. Now count the number of pieces of each type of material that you have collected. Put the results into your table.

Once you have recorded the results, you can plot them in a graph or chart. Think carefully about which kind of graph or chart would work best for your results.

Finally, look at the results table and the graph. What is the most common kind of trace evidence? What is least common? What else can you say about the data you have collected?

Safety first

Once you have finished checking your samples, wash your hands carefully, to minimize the risk of picking up any harmful microbes (germs) from the dust and dirt.

Timeline

The following timeline shows the steps that can occur when investigators look into the cause of a death.

Hour 0	Police enter the Boyds' flat and discover bodies.
30 minutes	The crime scene manager arrives.
Hour 1	SoCOs arrive and begins to photograph the scene.
	The medical examiner arrives.
Hour 2	An ambulance removes the bodies. SoCOs begin to collect evidence.
Hour 6	The last of the SoCOs leave the crime scene. The crime scene remains sealed off.
Hour 12	Police detectives are appointed.
	The evidence that the SoCOs collected is sent to the forensics lab.
Day 2	Door-to-door interviews in the neighbourhood begin.
	A pathologist carries out autopsies. He sends off blood samples and other evidence to the forensics lab.
	The forensics lab receives crime scene evidence.
Day 3	Investigators continue interviews and begin research into the Boyds and their lives.
Day 4	Biological samples from the autopsies arrive at the forensics lab.
Day 10	Results of blood tests and other tests from the autopsies are revealed. There is evidence of Rohypnol in the victims' blood.
Day 15	A firearms report is received, showing that two guns were used in the crime.
Day 21	Initial DNA results show that one blood sample has an unknown DNA profile.

Day 25	Trace evidence analysis takes place in the forensics lab, including an examination of evidence found on the wine glass.
	Investigators begin collecting saliva samples from the Boyds' relatives and neighbours.
	The third victim (Esteban) recovers consciousness. A police investigator interviews him.
Day 26	Investigators discuss Esteban's evidence. They begin to check into this evidence.
Day 29	Saliva samples are collected for a final day, and these samples are sent for DNA analysis. One man runs instead of giving a sample.
Day 33	The runaway man is caught, and his saliva is sent for urgent DNA testing.
Day 36	Results of the runaway man's DNA profile reveal that he is not connected to the murder, but he is a wanted bank robber.
Day 43	Results of DNA samples from neighbours show a match found with the "unknown" DNA from the crime scene.
Day 45	Police search the flat of the Boyds' upstairs neighbours. They find trace evidence.
Day 50	Analysis shows that the fibres and blood spots on the neighbours' clothing are from the crime scene. Police arrest the suspects.
Day 52	In a preliminary court hearing, the suspects are held for trial.
Month 8	The trial begins.

Glossary

adrenaline also called epinephrine. It is a hormone produced by the adrenal glands (two glands on top of the kidneys). It prepares the body for action, such as increasing the heart rate and releasing glucose into the blood.

antigen any substance that sets off an immune response in the body

assessment in a crime scene, an assessment is looking at the crime scene and making decisions such as which areas should be part of the crime scene, what evidence needs to be collected, and what needs to be done first

autopsy medical examination carried out on a dead person to try to determine the cause of death

ballistics study of the flight of bullets and other projectiles

barrister lawyer who acts as a prosecutor or defender in court cases

blood group doctors classify blood into several different types or blood groups, based on chemical markers called antigens found on the blood cells

calibre measurement of the size of a gun barrel, and so the size of ammunition it can fire

chromosome genetic material in a living cell. In most cells, chromosomes are found in the nucleus.

circulatory system organ system that circulates blood around the body. It consists mainly of the heart, arteries, capillaries, and veins.

contaminate contaminating a crime scene means to spoil the evidence by bringing in material from outside

CSI stands for "crime scene investigation"

decompose decay or rot

DNA genetic material of nearly all living things

DNA fingerprinting analysis of short sections of DNA (genetic material) to produce a DNA profile that is unique (except in the case of identical twins)

enzyme protein that speeds up chemical reactions inside cells. Each enzyme acts on a very specific chemical reaction or reactions.

evidence facts, information, or physical objects that are used to prove the truth of a hypothesis

forensics use of scientific tests in the investigation of crimes

genetic material genetic material is the substance that passes on inherited characteristics from one generation to the next

gland small body organ that is specialized to produce secretions (liquids that are released into the blood or other areas)

glucose sugar that acts as the main energy source for body cells

haematologist scientist who studies blood

hormone chemical that is produced from a gland in the body and released into the blood. The hormone travels in the blood to one or more target sites, where it has an effect.

hypothesis suggestion about what might have happened in a situation, based on limited evidence, that is used as the basis for further investigation

medical examiner doctor who works for the government and investigates unusual or suspicious deaths. Medical examiners carry out postmortem examinations.

nerve bundle of living fibres that carries information to or from the brain or the spinal cord as electrical impulses

nervous system organ system that carries nerve signals (electrical messages) to and from the brain or the spinal cord

pathologist doctor who studies the nature of diseases and their causes. A forensic pathologist carries out autopsies to find the cause of death.

pigment coloured chemical

public prosecutor law officer who acts against criminals on behalf of the state or in the public's interest

pulse regular throbbing in the arteries as the heart pushes blood through the circulatory system. The pulse can be felt in the wrist and the neck and can be used to measure the heart rate.

residue something remaining or left over, often after a chemical or physical process. For example, a salty residue is left after boiling seawater dry.

respiratory system organ system that brings oxygen into the blood system and allows carbon dioxide to escape into the air. It consists of the nose, mouth, windpipe, and lungs.

saliva liquid produced by glands in the mouth to soften food and begin the process of digestion

Scene of Crime Officer (SoCO) person who investigates crime scenes, looking for evidence that can later be used to prosecute a suspect

sedative drug that is taken for its calming or sleep-inducing effects

suicide when someone takes their own life

tissue group of cells within the body that work together for the same purpose. Examples are muscle tissue and epithelial tissue.

toxicology scientific study of drugs, poisons, and toxins

trace evidence material such as soil, pollen, fibres, or paint found in very small quantities at the scene of a crime

Find out more

Books

Crime Scene Investigator, Paul Millen (Constable & Robinson, 2008)

Crime Scene Investigators (Graphic Forensic Science), Rob Shone (Franklin Watts, 2008)

Crime Scenes: Revealing the Science Behind the Evidence, Paul Roland (Arcturus, 2006)

Famous Forensic Cases (Amazing Crime Scene Science), John Townsend (Franklin Watts, 2012)

Searching for Murder Clues (Amazing Crime Scene Science), John Townsend (Franklin Watts, 2012)

The Mammoth Book of New CSI, Nigel Cawthorne (Constable & Robinson, 2012)

Websites

www.bbc.co.uk/science/humanbody/body
Learn about the human body on the BBC's website.

www.forensic-science-society.org.uk/home
The Forensic Science Society has more information about the role of forensics in crime.

https://nationalcareersservice.direct.gov.uk/advice/planning/jobprofiles/Pages/scenesofcrimeofficer.aspx
If you want to know more about what a SoCO does and what qualifications you need to become one, visit the National Career Service's website.

welcometobaltimorehon.com/places/museumsattractions/the-nutshell-studies-of-unexplained-death
Find out more about the Nutshell Studies of Unexplained Death, the miniature crime scenes made in the 1940s to help pathologists and detectives investigate real crimes.

Topics to research: investigative careers

There are many different careers in crime scene investigation:

- SoCOs (UK) and CSIs (US) are police investigators who work on crime scenes. In the UK, they must have good GCSEs and A-levels. They also need good photographic ability: a qualification in photography is helpful.

- Forensic scientists process evidence collected by SoCOs. Forensic scientists must have a science degree, and many also do a postgraduate qualification in forensic science. Different types of scientist specialize in different areas. For example, biological scientists work on DNA and blood analysis, while drug analysts are usually chemists and ballistics experts are likely to be trained in physics.

- Medical examiners are often GPs who specialize in police work. Forensic pathologists are trained surgeons.

- Police detectives start as police officers. They do a combination of training courses and on-the-job training to develop their careers as detectives.

Index